MINDFULNESS

REWIRE YOUR REALITY

DIYA GUPTA

Contents

Contents

Introduction

The journey we experience and the circumstances we encounter daily, shape the exasperating emotions that bubble up in our mind, which can often attack our conscious, known as 'Mental Health'. Firstly, I'd like to introduce myself, I'm Diya Gupta, a 16 year old student. Since a young age I've experienced anxiety and soon with determination overcame it. This book represents my journey through anxiety and a weight on my mental health. This short book aims to spread awareness, and encourages strugglers to build their journey of hope. The book covers four sections of my journey, Stress & Anxiety, Change, Happiness, and Strength. By conducting my research I have enabled myself to understand other individuals and the relationships they build through their mental health journey.

1. STAY AWARE, HELP A FRIEND

Imagine, living in a world where your problems aren't accepted, belittled, and are labelled 'unimportant'. Stop imagining, because many people around the world go through that daily. Around 13% (970 million) of the world population encounters mental health issues, and from those 970 million strugglers more than half are ostracised from society and don't get their required treatment. Due to the lack of education on this subject and stereotypes, mental illnesses are still considered a stigma. These mental illnesses include depression, anxiety, eating disorders, schizophrenia, and adoptive addictions. Not many of us understand the cruel circumstances of these diseases that almost anyone can adopt. People can do the simplest gestures to help, the first step being acceptance and respect, as well as educating ourselves on this topic with reliable resources. We don't realize how many lives can be saved and changed. Be there for your loved ones.

2. BREATHE IN, BREATHE OUT

Make sure you're in an undisturbed environment. Get in a comfortable position, you could be lying down on the floor or bed, accompanied with a pillow or blanket. Be careful you're not forcing this exercise upon yourself, this could cause more stress. Ensure your body is ready to loosen up. Repeat the following exercise to your liking and preference.

- Inhale gently and deeply through your nose. Your abdomen should expand, and your chest must rise slightly.

- Exhale gently through your mouth. As you exhale air from your mouth, tighten your lips a little, make sure your jaw is relaxed. You may hear a soun of 'whooshing' as you exhale.

- Repeat this excercise as often as needed. You may do it a few times until you feel better.

STRESS & ANXIETY

3. Overthinking

Tangled thoughts and missile massacre is abruptly the same,
The act of murdering thoughts in the name of thinking is a flame,

Playing with yourself and swapping simultaneously between murder and victim
is solely overkilling,

These aren't tangled thoughts or complicit faults, it's overthinking
The sole cause of the demise of the brain.

4. Antagonist

I can feel the temper anguishing through my veins,
Tying my compelling thoughts in twirled chains,

Thoughts bursting inside like destructive fireworks ready to be played,
Words manipulating to a spherical steel body to rupture like a grenade,

Oh, how much I want to shatter you into bits and pieces,
Oh, how I hallucinated you to be cohesive,

My eyes dribble down blistering tears,
You made me regret all that was here,

5. Anger vs Anger

Her palm interlocks its adjacent clone into a fist,
The fist beholds not only molested sweat seeping through the fingers but a
forsaken story,

A story with steady rage and knot choking betrayal,
The determined rampage of fury manipulates into a damn bursting into a well
of tears,

A feeling quite condemn and independent,
The solemn heart shatters with the last fragile breathe, losing it all for none at
all

6. Anxiety

Pulled down to the floor,

Twist and turn through the doors, Restlessness crawl to the toes,

Sleep tucked in a heavy chest, Breathless thoughts are gasps,

Folded into a box, dimensions are lost,

Quickening through the pulse, Dreams smothered to dust,

A sinking sensation, I'm left to drown,

The emotions are numb, I can't hear a sound,

7. Isolation

The loneliness creeps up my stiff shoulders,
Escaping the timidness in the stale atmosphere,

The walls aggravate closer to my hollow chest,
Suppressing the buried emotions,
My inner conscience entangled in procrastination,

Expectations slowly seeping into reality,
Empathy closing its doors to motivation,
And then it was just me,
and only me

8. In or Out

The doors are collapsing, slamming one by one,
A faint scream of my inner temperament, signaling a success catastrophe,
The pathway of life seeming to encounter misplaced stones,
The mind intended a forsaken destination of darkness, but the heart had the zeal to enlighten,

9. Aftermath

The fresh green breeze stumbles upon my nose,
The lost feeling of that scent had gone over the bridges to a forsaken land,

The sky accumulated only days of blue,
no marshmallow swirls, only poofs of grey

The anxiously chirping birds hover no more,
No children's playful cheers, only the production of industrial beers,

The clouds smile with defeat,
dwelling the darkness and the long lost summer breeze,

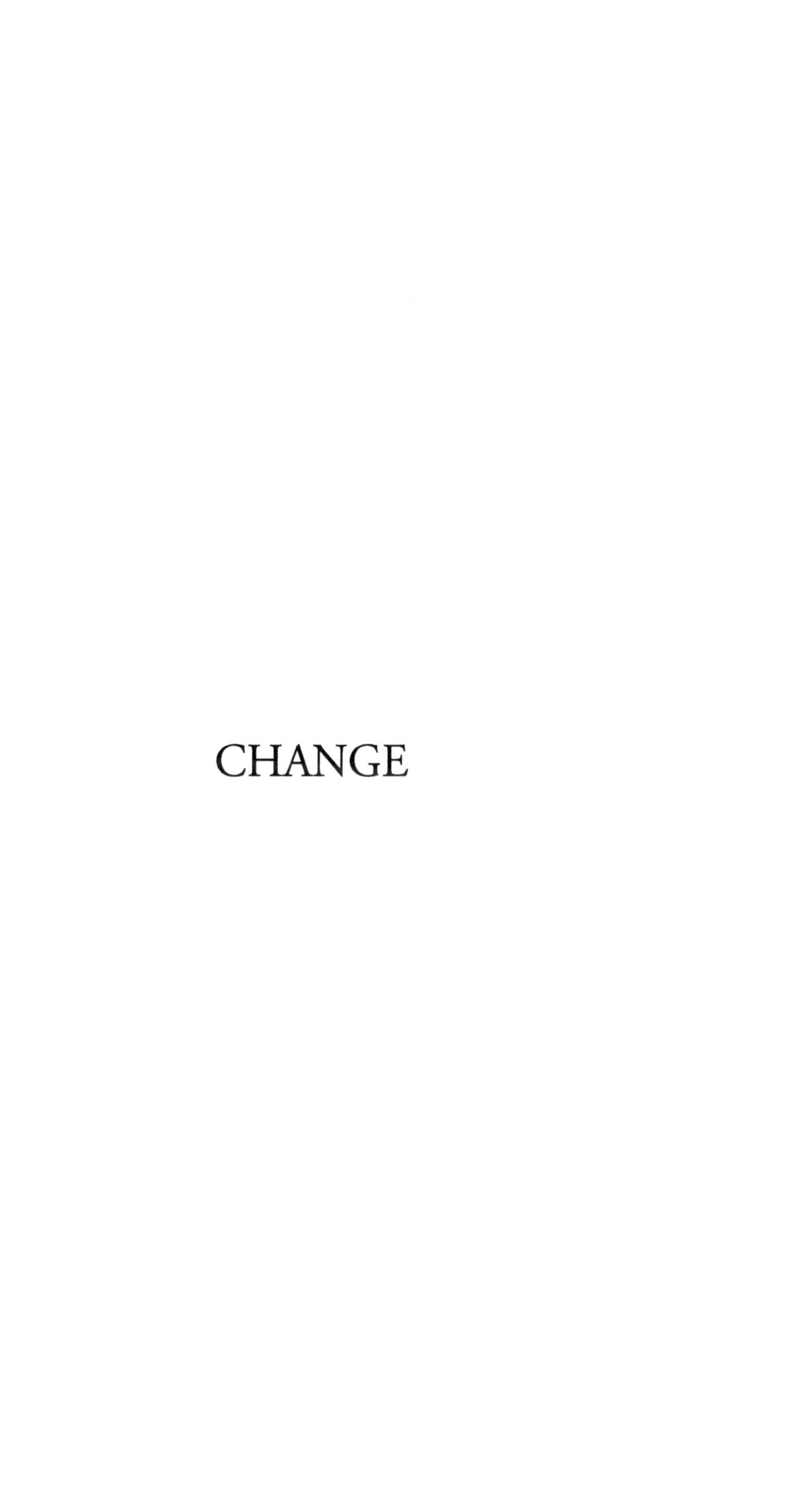

CHANGE

10. Kids

We believed like we were vulnerable,
We believed every word of hope,

We were happy, we laughed,
Sadness didn't last too long for us,

Our souls didn't believe in misery,
We were lost in our dreams not giving up,

We were entangled to the comfort of our heart,

Promises vowed as real commitments,
But then we grew up,

11. Growing Up

Somewhere between 'Ignoring' and 'Forgiving', we grew up!

Somewhere between 'cribbing' and 'Adjusting' we grew up!

Somewhere between 'Puppy love' and 'Tinder' we grew up!

Somewhere between 'I want to be an adult' and 'I want to be a child again', we grew up!

Somewhere between '1 aed for 10 candies' and '10 aed for 1 candy', we grew up!

Somewhere between 'Crying for attention' and 'Smiling so the tears don't fall', we grew up!

Somewhere between 'Best Friends Forever' and 'Fake friends', we grew up!

Somewhere between 'Catch me if you can' and 'Gyming', we grew up!

Somewhere between 'Being loved' and 'To love', we grew up!

inspired by Manvi Bhatia

12. It took over

Those moments of glee,
They made me,

Collecting them one by one,
All the moments of pleasure and fun,

They were Guarded with an invisible string around my heart,

To never let go, they're more precious than treasure,

Each vein keeping them alive, they never died Bones
tingling with nostalgia,

My heartwarming up and a soft smile gliding across my face,

It was the memories that took over again,

13. Fake Friends

Whisper, whispers, whispers,
Gasps, Gasps, Gasps
Chuckles, chuckles, chuckles

They make friendship sound stale,
With their audacious trail,
There were unnecessary conversations,
No emotional relationships,
You call me when you need glee,
Shut me out when you've used me,

They were forced interactions,
With hidden brutal actions,
Never lost a friend,
Never really had one,

14. So far way

Your hand in mine,
we're watching the northern lights,

You ask me what's my greatest fear,
I answered "not having this"
You shrug with a soft grin,

A year later
We're at the departures gate,
You ask me what's my greatest fear,
I answer "this"
You shrug with a soft grin,
And leave.

15. 2020

Never would we have imagined toasting a new year to a decade of uncertainty,

For most, this was a year of refreshment,
more so a decade of important milestones,

This unexpected start is moreover a learning curve,
how to adapt and be grateful,

This isn't a year of a disappointment,
this is a year of growth,

We're rejoicing family relations,
fulfilling the main objective of technology,

Many are struggling too, but many are empathizing with community service to
the needy,
We're all in this together!

HAPPINESS

16. First Love

Our eyes collide with a hint of unraveling trouble,
Butterflies invade my stomach so swiftly,

Your hands cuddle my heart so tightly,
my heart escapes a beat so wisely,

The warmth that this love brings, is immense beyond words,
I think I'm in love,aroused with the sensation of a blooming rose,

In your presence, my half heart feels complete,like a jigsaw puzzle,
My love, your eyes behold the mystery that I'm willing to undercover,

You've made my heart smile and eyes shine,
'You're mine',forever echoes majestically through my heart,

I love you.

17. Siblings

They'll have a salty fight or two till their heart runs out of the dew,
They'll criticize till the other gains mountains of new,
They'll stand like an army around the adolescent heart of the other,
They'll annoy another till the other screams "Mother!",
They share a beautiful bond of love and trust which is young, fulfilled and full of love,

18. Blur

The tenacious towers swirl to a complicit blur,
The lights squint to a twilight lure,
The city vibrates with rowdy lanes and clinks of glasses go cheers,
The city's mellowness contemplates with the rock of the car gears,
The city life adds more color to the night sky than the sun,

19. Summer

The sea is blue with the light cream waves
twirling towards you,

The legs are descending in the soggy sand,
the feet coming closer to land,

The sun sizzling my sandy wet hair,
crisping into curls of rare,

A refreshing lemonade by the pool,
the ice melting swiftly prompting the cup to drool,

The warmth of the flaky sunscreen dissolving into my skin,
like a blanket within,

The summer shades are on to tackle the brightness,
maintaining the natural lightness,

Freedom in the humid air,
no school and more time to spare,

20. Vanilla

Lying down by the meddling paths of the meadow,
Hallucinating about you like a beau,

Your fine dreamy white glazed tier,
Bringing my heart a scintillating cheer,

The reward you bring to my pallet with grace,
The first lick is compatible to love at first taste,

Oh, how simple you are yet I devour,
Making me feel more than empowered,

Oh, vanilla I can't wait till we meet,
As I open your box to endure this sweet treat

21. Long Way Home

The sun says goodbye behind the wanderlust
waves of the cloud built beach,

The tranquil spirit of the rain partnering up
with the thankful clouds it seems,

It's a long way home on this meddling path
that leads to nowhere and everywhere,

It's a path of possibilities and liberties through
the path of infinity,
The car bickering by speed, the wipers
swishing through the glass that gleams,

It's a long way home accompanying the
heavenly view of the compeer old team

STRENGTH

22. Her

Only words hurt her in the typhoon of life,
Her scars were her identity,
her strength, her pride,

The endings seemed new beginnings to her,
She was the society's reproval but her self's approval,

Her perspective mattered more than others objective,
She only looked down to glare at her shoes not to blur out her views,

She lived, laughed, loved and died

23. The Upper Lord

Some believe he's the twinkle of the stars,
Some pray that he's the wealth of their cars,
Some believe he's within us till eternity,
Some believe he's the one who makes these fraternities,
Some don't believe and think ignorance is bliss,
But God has no limit or boundaries and is the one to dismiss,
We all know that God indeed has a marvelous plan that awaits,

24. New-ness

Locking my eyes with my eyelids,
Blocking my ears with numbness,
Pursing my lips with unspoken words,

The smell of hope fainting distantly,
Isolating myself with my thoughts,
Gasping for submerged ingenuity,

Then I met you,
The feeling of warmth returned,
A new lens of light was the key,
My heart blossomed with sunshine,

There was comfort within my thoughts,
My weaknesses became my strength,
Until someone else needed it more than I did,

25. The Road Not Taken

I'll climb the ladder,
The ladder of hope,

Disappointing every father,
I'll try harder to not mope,
I may not surpass,
the anticipated feeling,

But I will avoid the emasculated kneeling,

These expectations may drop,
But I'll forever rise,

In the eyes of the road not taken,
I'll make my way through despise

26. Battle with yourself

The soldiers trudge in agitation along the rotten
graveyard,

Holding great resemblance between an unwilled hag,

Fighting the battle for a conflicted superior,

The superior that is a lonesome,
coward bloke,

A superior that holds no value of diplomacy,

The art of peace and negotiation,

Badgering to the death the people of the hogged
land, to win the battle

Simultaneously killing their inner conscience with
every dagger,

Half the battle is won after peace is commended with
ourselves,

Which took the lonesome bloke quite the time to
conquest,

27. Peace with oneself and the sea

The fear of sinking in this deep blue
magnet seems tremendous,

The overlapping shades of each wave merge
to a circle of foam,

The risk is greater but the hope is as a
solvent to the debts of reality,

The freedom rims in with periwinkle while
the risk is left behind with the sapphire
tier,

The inner peace passes understanding as
the gushing sea fills it with no more than
tranquility,

let go, breathe.

Trust yourself.

*'You've survived a lot,
and you'll survive whatever
is coming.'*

–Robert Tew